Eating well on a Budget

AGE CONCERN
IN ASSOCIATION WITH
THE BBC FOOD & DRINK
PROGRAMME

ACKNOWLEDGEMENTS

Age Concern would like to thank the following people:
Mr and Mrs Brand and Chef Michael Quinn for providing the essential ingredients of enthusiasm and time in devising and tasting the recipes.
The Food & Drink programme, particularly Tracey MacLeod, for help in producing this book based on an item from their programme.

Nutritional and budgeting guidelines written by Carol Leverkus

Edited by Lee Bennett

Designed by Eugenie Dodd

Printed by Eyre & Spottiswoode, The Grosvenor Press, Portsmouth

Cover photograph by Anthony Blake

© 1987 Age Concern England
Bernard Sunley House
60 Pitcairn Road
Mitcham, Surrey CR4 3LL

ISBN 086242 053-9

All rights reserved, no part of this work may be reproduced in any form by mimeograph or any other means, without permission in writing from the publisher.

CONTENTS

PAGE **4** Introduction

6 Eating what you fancy?

12 Shopping on a budget

15 Cooking and storing food

18 The Brands' menu

INTRODUCTION

My ingenuity as a chef was put to the test by the BBC 'Food & Drink' Programme when I was asked in the autumn of 1986 to devise a menu for a week for a retired couple with £25 to spend on food. Many pensioners are deprived of the enjoyment food can provide as a result of high prices and because they may also not know how to get the best results from simple food. The challenge for me was to add a little luxury style to the way food is prepared.

With the help of pensioners Doris and Frank Brand from Exeter, the recipes from page 20 were successfully cooked and tasted on the programme. For people new to cooking, recipes for simple dishes like rice pudding have also been included. The Brands were excited with the results of their cooking and of course delighted that they had kept within their budget.

Although the figure of £25 was selected as an average amount for a couple to spend who live on the basic pension, the circumstances of other pensioners with expensive housing, heating or travel costs may reduce their food budget below the suggested level. Also this amount could leave you with little to spend on the extra frills if you have a larger than average appetite, if you need a special diet or if you can only get to the more expensive local shops to buy your food. The Food & Drink Programme costed all ingredients in line with prices in the shops.

As the nutritional side of the Brands' menu was another essential, the recipes chosen were based on wholesome ingredients. To explain more about healthy eating, the nutritionist Carol Leverkus has included guidelines in addition to editing the recipes for their nutritional value and giving her tips on budgeting.

Preparing and cooking food can be a pleasurable activity, when you're retired and have the time to extend your skills on recipes like the stuffed chicken legs on page 35, as Frank and Doris did. "We've tried these several times. When you are actually shown how to cook something in a new way and you put your mind to it, you'll find it quite easy."

Eating well on a tight budget is all down to good planning, wise shopping and a good dollop of common sense.

Michael Quinn, MBE
*Ettington Park Hotel
Alderminster,
Warwickshire*

EATING WHAT YOU FANCY?

A little of what you fancy does you good. With all the talk today on what you should be eating for the sake of good health, it's still worth remembering this familiar saying. Eating should be fun, so cooking 'something special' is particularly important during retirement when meals readily become the focus of the day.

However, to enjoy that hard-earned retirement to the full, good health is a vital ingredient which is dependent on the skilful selection of food at a time of life when people become more 'at risk' in terms of their diet, inspite of years of experience in choosing and preparing food.

Choosing healthy food

Even though the amount of energy (ie calories) needed from food decreases with age, the body's requirements for essential vitamins, minerals and other nutrients is little altered. As no group of foods contains all the nutrients required, you need to choose from a variety of foods, and avoid excesses, as outlined in these two rules.

1
Plan your meals to include:
a vegetable and/or fruit; some fish, cheese, meat, eggs, dried beans, lentils or nuts; and to fill up on – some bread, crispbread, potato, rice and spaghetti. Aim to eat regularly with a mixture of hot and cold meals.

2
Choose whole foods such as:
wholemeal bread and other wholegrain cereals, vegetables, lentils and beans, fruit, fish and lean meats rather than highly processed foods full of fats, sugar, salt and lots of additives.

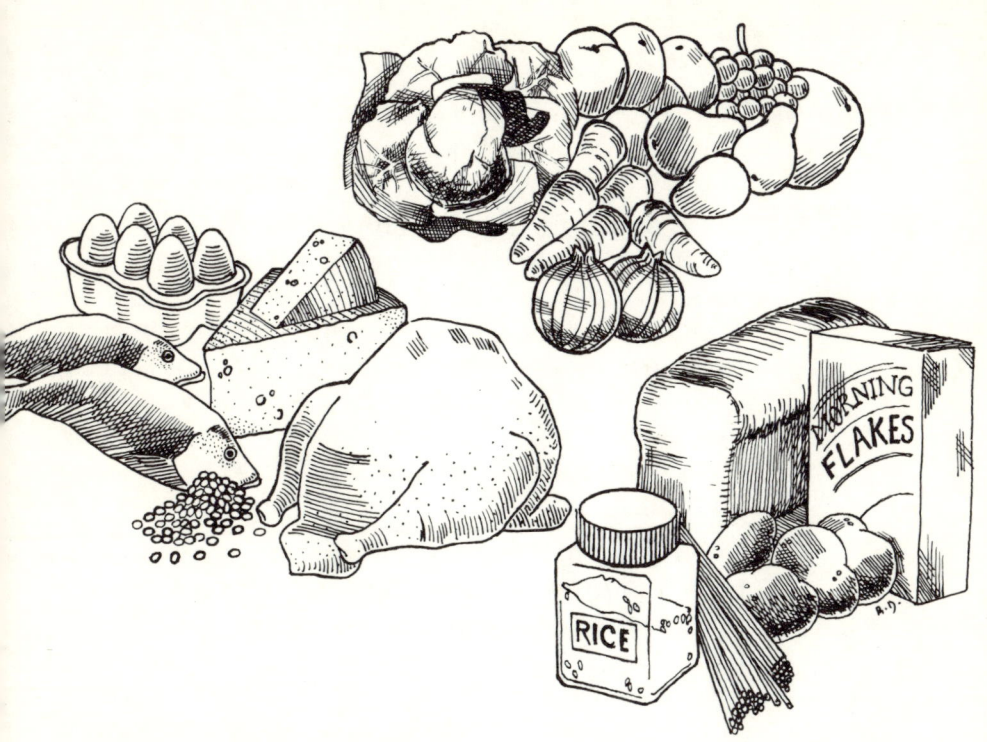

For Vitamin D and Calcium

These are required to maintain strong healthy bones. Vitamin D is usually obtained from sunlight, but anyone staying indoors for long periods can go short of it, unless a proper food source is chosen. Additional Calcium may be needed by women from late middle age to prevent weak and brittle bones.

Sources of Calcium:
Milk, cheese, yogurt
Canned fish (with bones)
Bread, flour
Hard water

Sources of Vitamin D:
Oily fish (mackerel, pilchards, sardines, herring, tuna)
Eggs
Margarine, some natural yogurts, evaporated milk, Ovaltine
Cornflakes (check the labelling for details)

For Vitamin C, Folic Acid and Iron

Folic Acid is a B Vitamin and along with Vitamin C and Iron helps to maintain healthy blood and prevent anaemia and tiredness. Vitamin C helps the iron in food to be absorbed. Folic acid is also essential in the formation of the body's cells, which make up our tissues, and helps prevent fatigue and depression. These two vitamins need special attention because they are easily destroyed, are not stored in the body for long and their main sources usually require regular shopping.

Even though, it can seem an unnecessary effort to cook and prepare vegetables for just yourself or one other person, for the sake of good health, make that effort. When cooking, use the minimum amount of water for the shortest possible time. Try to eat some vegetables raw as salad most days.

What about the question of fresh or frozen vegetables? They are best straight from the fields; but when fresh means a few days old, then nutritionally speaking, good quality frozen ones are just as good or better. To get value for money, fresh vegetables and fruits in season should be your first choice, using frozen ones occasionally for convenience and when fresh are scarce and expensive. Tinned and dried vegetables are nutritionally inferior but make a good standby. For example, using tinned tomatoes makes sound sense during the winter when locally grown ones are unavailable.

Vegetarian diets can be very healthy, but plenty of non-meat sources of iron, such as those listed below should be eaten to prevent anaemia.

Sources of Vitamin C:
Citrus fruits (oranges, grapefruit, satsumas and their juices)
Other fruits like berries, fresh pineapple, bananas
Vegetables – fresh or frozen – (cabbage, sprouts, greens, cauliflower, new potatoes, tomatoes)

Sources of Folic Acid:
Green vegetables, parsnips
Egg yolk
Liver, kidney
Yeast, and meat extracts
Pulses (peas, dried beans, lentils)
Fruits (oranges, bananas, melon)

Sources of Iron:
Red meat, especially liver and kidney
Liver sausage
Pulses, green vegetables
Breads and cereals, especially wholegrain
Cocoa
Eggs

For Fibre

It helps prevent constipation and other intestinal disorders such as diverticular disease and piles. Because fibre-rich foods are filling, they help you avoid eating too many calories, which add weight. In addition, fibre is a good source of nutrients like folic acid, vitamins, iron and other minerals. Fibre is very important for our health in spite of being the part of food not absorbed by the body.

When increasing the amount of fibre in your diet, let your body adjust by doing this gradually.
By eating plenty of the fibre-rich foods mentioned below, you will get all the fibre you need without having to add bran to your food. You will also get all the nutrients which bran does not provide.

Sources of Fibre:
Wholegrain breads, crispbreads	Wholegrain rice, spaghetti, macaroni
Wholegrain and bran cereals	Fruits, vegetables (peas, beans and lentils)
Oats, barley, rye	Nuts, seeds

Sweet and fatty foods?

As you need fewer calories as you get older, remember that sugar and fat provide calories in a concentrated form. Advising you to eat extra wholemeal bread, potatoes and rice may sound strange, as once upon a time these were the foods slimmers were advised to cut out. Eating these filling foods helps you to cut down on fattening and less nourishing cakes, high-fat cheeses, butter, fried foods, pies and sweetened drinks.

Which kind of fat?

When planning your meals remember there are two kinds of fat, saturated and unsaturated. Choose the healthier polyunsaturates we hear about so frequently these days, which are a form of unsaturated fat. Apart from leading to overweight, too much saturated fat in your diet raises the cholesterol level in the arteries which causes heart disease.

Sources of saturated fats:
Full-fat milk, cream	Meat products (pies, salami, pâté, sausages)
Most hard and full-fat cream cheeses	Cakes, biscuits
Butter, lard, dripping, suet	Fried foods, chips

Good alternatives:

Semi-skimmed or skimmed milk	Lean mince, reduced-fat sausages and pâtés, offal, chicken and turkey (skin removed)
Natural yogurt, reduced-fat creams	
Reduced-fat hard cheeses, Edam, Cottage cheese, curd cheese, low-fat soft cheeses	Breads and scones made with polyunsaturated fat
	Polyunsaturated margarine or low-fat spread
Fish – fresh or tinned (drained of oil)	Corn or soya oils

Watch out for sugar

Eating too many sweet foods is not just a matter of concern if you are overweight. Sugar encourages tooth decay and gum disease and provides empty calories – that is, fattening ones without other valuable nutrients. You don't need sugar for energy, as all food provides it; and you will get all you need from other healthy food.

Sources of sugar:
Packet sugar used in cooking and at the table
Cakes and biscuits
Sweets and chocolates
Soft and alcoholic drinks
Canned fruit in syrup
Fruit yogurts

Good alternatives:
Artificial sweeteners
Homemade breads and scones made with little or no sugar
Fresh or dried fruit
Unsalted nuts
Low-calorie, 'dry' alcoholic drinks, mineral water
Fruit canned in natural juice
Yogurts without added sugar

SHOPPING ON A BUDGET

The tips given below will apply to some of you more than others, depending on how near you live to a supermarket or a street market, whether you have transport for shopping and your access to home-grown vegetables and fruits. If you live alone, obviously the amount of food you could buy from a supermarket would not warrant the expense of a long bus or taxi fare; and you will have to continue using your local shops.

- Plan meals around nutritious foods which give value for money:
  Fish (tinned), milk, yogurt, cheese, eggs; pulses (dried beans, peas, lentils); offal; chicken; wholemeal bread; oats, rice, spaghetti, macaroni; potatoes, vegetables; fruit juice (long-life cartons); margarine, corn and soya oils.

- Roughly plan your meals for a few days ahead for two advantages. Firstly, you need a shopping list which, if adhered to, prevents expensive impulse buys. Secondly, you can avoid waste by basing meals on the same ingredients but by varying their texture and taste, as shown in The Brands' menu on pages 18-19.

- Choose basic and unprocessed foods which are cheaper and more nutritious (oats, corn and wheat flakes for cereals) a bacon hock to cook rather than a veal and ham pie.

- Buy the supermarket 'own brands' to save money; and get accustomed to the 'best buys' offered in local shops. Ham or some cheese may be competitive in one shop and tinned foods in another.

- Check the weight for the price given on a packet of a particular brand. It can be helpful to have a small calculator at hand as packaging can be so misleading. Sometimes smaller packs on special offer work out cheaper than larger ones.

- Avoid gimmicky packaging or food sold in special health or festive sections – these products usually have a higher mark-up and give poor value for money.

- Read food labels carefully to see what you are paying for. Terms like 'chicken flavour' or 'strawberry flavour' can be very misleading and do not mean you will find chicken or strawberry in the food.

- Markets are usually good for fresh fruit, vegetables, wet fish and eggs; but get to know one or two reliable stalls. Beware of inferior quality (citrus fruits that are showing signs of mould; tomatoes or a cauliflower with black patches). If you don't like the look of the item you have been given, be firm and ask for a better one. Also, remember when items like Bramleys, celery and corn on the cob are in season and at their cheapest.

- Learn the days and times that certain perishables (chicken pieces, fish, red meat, yogurt or cream) are reduced for quick sale. Plan shopping expeditions to coincide with these times, but work your menu around the perishable items. They need to be eaten without delay once they have reached their 'sell-by' date.

- Make use of special offers to stock up your store cupboard (tinned tomatoes or fruit sold cheaper when fresh produce is in season). Check the 'sell-by' dates and quality of the products.

- When planning different meals, based on the same product (allowing you to buy larger more economical packs), look for the latest 'sell-by' date. This saves you from throwing away the remainder before you can use it for a second or third meal.

- Look for broken pieces or off-cuts of ham and bacon, cheese for cooking, broken nuts; smaller apples or prunes or dried apricot pieces.
- Be aware that cheapest is not always the best value. Lean mince or reduced-fat sausages are healthier and better value, as there is little fat to discard.
- Share large packs with neighbours or friends. This is particularly useful for fruits and vegetables from the market, cereals and bread.

COOKING AND STORING FOOD

In suggesting the Brands' menu on pages 18-19, Michael Quinn stressed the importance of planning and avoiding waste – both of fuel and food.

- When your main weekly shopping is done, sit down and plan your meals for a few days ahead. Think about what will remain from one meal that can be kept and carefully stored for another. What about the vegetable trimmings, stock from boiling meat or vegetables? It's cheaper to buy a whole chicken or an economical joint like a hock and stretch it over two or three meals.

- When adapting to cooking for fewer people and smaller appetites, avoid preparing too much. To keep from going over your budget, be strict about reducing the quantities in recipes. Only cook extra when you have planned to carefully store the surplus for another meal.

- It might be difficult to have as much variety from day to day when basing several meals on the same meat or vegetable. If this is so, create change from week to week to excite your taste buds.

- When using the same ingredient for consecutive meals, create interest by varying the texture, the colour and the type of meal. See, for example, the use of leftover bacon in the recipe on page 24.

- The following vegetables are all valuable for single or small households as they store reasonably well when kept cool: beetroot, carrots, celery, chicory, Chinese Leaf, courgettes, Dutch cabbage, garlic, Iceberg lettuce, leeks, marrow, onions, potatoes, swede, turnip. Celery, for example, can be used in salad, braised and served on its own, or used to flavour soup or a stuffing, as for the recipe on page 32. For another week, different meals could be based on cabbage. Nonetheless, the fresher, the better for both taste and nutritional quality.

- Cooking a little of two vegetables and serving them together gives extra colour and interest to a meal (peas and cabbage or carrots and celery).
- Most dishes can be given that extra touch by making good use of herbs, spices, freshly ground pepper and a cider or wine vinegar. (Avoid malt vinegar which kills the flavour of food – other than for poaching eggs).
- Keep some of the following in the store cupboard:

  curry powder, cayenne or paprika, black pepper; cloves, mixed spice, cinnamon, vanilla essence; dried fruit, brown or demerara sugar; tomato purée, garlic, stock cubes, wine or cider vinegar; mixed herbs and your favourite ones (tarragon, chervil, basil, thyme); duty-free cooking or local brandy or rum, sherry, cider, beer.

  Remember that herbs and spices quickly lose their punch, so buy small quantities. If you can, grow and dry your own, even in a tub indoors.
- If cost is a barrier to cooking something new because you need to buy two or three extra items at one go, try to spread out the cost by squeezing one item into the shopping budget each week.
- Don't get hung up on following recipes exactly. You may find that one of the required ingredients is of poor quality or more expensive than you thought. There may be some leftovers to use up or there may be produce available in the garden or from a neighbour. Adapt recipes to your circumstances and taste. For example, you may wish to use some leeks instead of onions, peas for

their colour instead of green pepper or an ordinary grapefruit instead of a pink one.

- When using the oven, try to cook two or more items at once (see the menus for Saturday and Monday). Similarly, foods can be steamed over another item being cooked.

- Rather than keeping some cooked meat to serve for the next meal, you may prefer to cook double quantities of one dish and freeze half for another meal. But the food must *not* be re-frozen. Even with a three star freezer, three months should be the maximum storage time.

- Hygiene is important when using leftovers and reheating meals. Never reheat food twice. Cool stocks, meat and fish quickly and store in the fridge. Reheat them thoroughly. Never mix together raw and cooked ingredients for a dish while they are being stored.

- If you find it difficult to work in the kitchen for a long spell, do things in stages and prepare what you can the day before or earlier in the day. Don't be put off cooking the more time-consuming dishes in The Brands' menu. For example the stuffed chicken legs on page 35 could be prepared on Sunday evening ready for roasting for lunch on Monday.

THE BRANDS' MENU

■ Because Doris and Frank Brand like to shop on Wednesdays, they planned a week's menu starting on that day. In order to keep within their budget, Michael Quinn based his recipes on the principle of using one basic ingredient – like the bacon hock – for different meals on several days. Because the Brands preferred to have their main meal at mid-day, their menu has been presented that way; but it can be reversed to suit your taste.

WEDNESDAY

Mid-day Boiled bacon hock or knuckle
Braised rice with curried mixed vegetables
Lemon syllabub
Evening Split pea soup and bread

THURSDAY

Mid-day Braised red cabbage with ham, apples and steamed parsnips
Caramelised oranges
Evening Open sandwich with pâté and tomato

FRIDAY

Mid-day Fish (poached or grilled) and sautéd potatoes
Grapes with cream
Evening Tomato salad with stuffed eggs
Bread

SATURDAY

Mid-day Neck of lamb with lentils, peas and potato layer
Baked apple tart
Evening Baked sweetcorn with cheese sauce
Wholemeal toast

FROM MICHAEL QUINN'S SPECIAL RECIPES

■ The following items were included in the weekly budget of £25: continental breakfast, milk cereals, fruit juice, tea, sugar and condiments.

■ The quantities are for two people and suited the Brands' appetite.

SUNDAY

Mid-day Roast chicken with braised celery, parsnips and gravy
Baked rice pudding with jam
Cider to drink

Evening Cheese soufflé rarebit with salad
Fresh fruit

MONDAY

Mid-day Chicken legs stuffed with herbs and sausagemeat
Baked potatoes and green salad
Fruit en papillote

Evening Creamed carrot soup with grated Cheddar cheese
Wholemeal bread

TUESDAY

Mid-day Macaroni cheese with peppers and bacon
Peas and cabbage
Grilled grapefruit

Evening Cold chicken with cucumber yogurt salad
Wholemeal bread

WEDNESDAY

Boiled bacon hock or knuckle

1 bacon hock or knuckle joint
1 onion (4-5 ozs)
4 cloves
¼ pint cider

1. Stud onion with cloves (push sharp end of cloves into onion).
2. Place hock, onion and cider in a very large pan. Add enough water to cover hock.
3. Bring to boil and simmer until meat is tender – about 1 hour.
4. Take meat out of the pan and cut off enough for the meal.

Braised rice with curried mixed vegetables

2 oz long-grain rice (try wholemeal)
pepper to season
½ oz margarine
½ onion (2 oz)
⅔ pint chicken stock

1 courgette
1 leek
2 carrots
½ oz margarine
½ onion (2 oz)
dash tomato purée
1 teaspoon curry powder
1 teaspoon flour
1 tablespoon natural yogurt

Rice

1. Meanwhile, finely chop ½ onion.
2. Heat ½ oz margarine until just sizzling, using a small/medium pan with a lid.
3. Add onion and cook for 2 minutes, stirring occasionally.
4. Add rice seasoned with pepper.

WEDNESDAY

5   Stir around and add ⅔ pint warm chicken stock.
6   Fold a sheet of greaseproof paper to form a lid and place it over the rice mixture to trap the steam. Cover with pan lid.
7   Simmer on a very low heat gently for about 20 minutes – longer for brown rice – until soft. Every 5 minutes stir gently with fork to prevent rice sticking to bottom of pan. Replace greaseproof and lid each time. Never stir rice with a spoon.

Alternatively, the rice may be braised in a hot oven for 20 minutes, after bringing it to the boil on the stove.

8   When cooked, remove greaseproof, fluff up with a fork and leave to rest for 10-20 minutes, while finishing the preparation of the rest of the meal.

Vegetables 1   Top and tail courgette, leek and carrots, and cut into matchstick pieces with a sharp knife. Place in metal colander or sieve.
2   Just before serving the meal, steam the vegetables sticks for a few minutes over the hock (in the colander or sieve or wrapped in tin foil).

Mild curry sauce
1   Chop remaining ½ onion very finely.
2   Heat ½ oz margarine in a small pan and add onion. Cook for 2 minutes, stirring occasionally.
3   Add the dash of tomato purée and cook for another minute, followed by the curry powder, cooking for a further minute, giving a stir.
4   Stir in the flour and cook for another minute.
5   Stir in ½ pint of the bacon stock and cook for 20 minutes.
6   Take off the heat and stir in the yogurt.

WEDNESDAY

7 Pour over the chopped meat and serve with the vegetables and rice.

NOTES *Keep the remaining bacon stock in the refrigerator, for the evening's Split pea soup and Thursday's Braised red cabbage.*
Leftover ham is for Thursday's Braised red cabbage and should be stored in the refrigerator.

Lemon syllabub

1 lemon
½ small carton single cream
4 tablespoons yogurt
1 teaspoon caster sugar
1 tablespoon cooking brandy

1 Wash lemon and grate the peel into a 1 pint/small basin.
2 Roll lemon to help release juices.
3 Squeeze the juice from the halved lemon into basin.
4 Add remaining ingredients, mix and then whisk until fluffy.
5 Pour into two serving dishes and cool.
6 Optional decorations include a lemon slice and a mint leaf.

NOTES *Keep the remaining lemon and juice in the fridge for Saturday's apple tart and Tuesday's cucumber yogurt salad.*

WEDNESDAY

Split pea soup

1½ pints bacon stock (from boiled hock)
½lb/225g dried split peas
1 leek
1 stick celery
dash double cream
1 tablespoon chopped fresh or 1 teaspoon of dried parsley
seasoning

1 Wash celery and leek and slice finely.
2 Put them with the split peas in the cold stock.
3 Bring to the boil and simmer gently for about ¾ hour until peas are soft.
4 For a smooth soup, put in a blender or pass through a sieve. Otherwise serve as it comes.
5 To serve, pour into soup bowls, add a dash of cream, season to taste and sprinkle with chopped parsley.

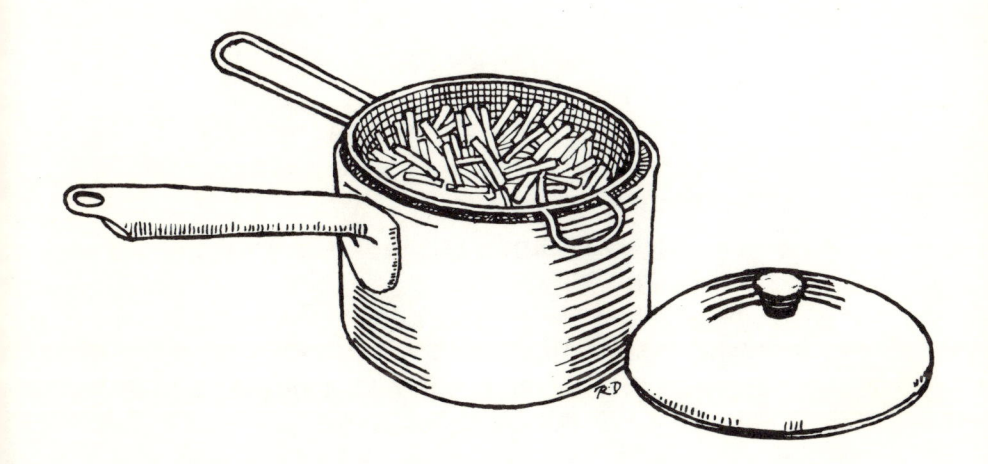

THURSDAY

Braised red cabbage with ham, apples and steamed parsnips

8 oz red cabbage (about ¼ cabbage)
2 oz/50g raisins
2 Bramley apples
1 flat tablespoon demerara sugar
2 tablespoons white wine or cider vinegar
1½ pints bacon stock (from hock)
leftover ham from the hock or knuckle
½ lb parsnips

1. Finely slice the washed cabbage.
2. Wash, peel (if desired) core and chop the apples.
3. Place cabbage and apples in a large pan (about 4 pints) with the raisins, sugar, vinegar and stock — first, removing any fat that has settled on the top. If a knuckle joint has been used for the stock instead of a bacon hock, season with salt.
4. Bring to the boil and cook gently on a very low heat for about 1½ hours stirring about ever 20 minutes.

   Alternatively, braise in the oven at about 300°F/150°C Gas 2 in a casserole dish, after first bringing mixture to the boil on the stove. If you prefer to use a pressure cooker, cabbage will braise in 25 minutes.
5. Clean the parsnips and cut into 4 wedge-shaped pieces.
6. For the last 20 minutes add the remaining meat from Wednesday's hock or knuckle joint, reheat thoroughly, while steaming the parsnips in a metal sieve, colander or tin foil.
7. Serve when nearly all the stock has evaporated.

THURSDAY

Caramelised oranges

1 large or 2 small oranges
1½ oz sugar

1. Top and tail orange.
2. Sit orange on its flat bottom and slice downwards around it with a sharp knife to remove skin and pith.
3. Slice orange across the segments and place in a heat-resistant bowl with any escaped juice.
4. Put nearly all the sugar in a small heavy bottomed pan and just cover with water.
5. Bring to the boil and then lower heat.
When starting to brown, shake pan slightly.
As soon as all the sugar has browned, pour over the oranges. Don't worry — it should sizzle.
6. Shred the peel into slithers as fine as possible.
7. Boil in a little water with remaining sugar.
8. Sprinkle cooked peel over the orange and syrup, adding a dash of brandy or liquor if available.
9. Leave in the fridge for at least one hour before serving. If the budget allows, this is delicious with a little ice-cream.

NOTE *For today's evening meal, make an open sandwich with low-fat pâté, from the delicatessen counter at your supermarket or butcher.*

FRIDAY

Fish (poached or grilled) with sautéd potatoes

For grilling:
1 large/2 small prepared mackerels or herrings

For poaching:
8 oz coley, milk, bay leaf, ¼ onion (optional)
2 potatoes
pinch rosemary
clove of garlic (optional)
4 tablespoons oil
seasoning

For grilling: Brush mackerel or herring with oil and season. Grill for about 15 minutes.

For poaching: Just cover fish in milk in covered pan, and for extra flavour, add ¼ onion and bay leaf. Simmer for about 5 minutes until cooked, but gently to prevent fish from breaking up.

Sautéd potatoes

1. While fish is cooking, wash or peel potatoes and slice. If they are fat, cut lengthwise as well.
2. Peel garlic, if desired, and chop finely.
3. Heat oil in a frying pan (preferably a non-stick one that requires less oil).
4. Add garlic and lightly fry, then add seasoned potatoes and rosemary.
5. Fry until potatoes are cooked, stirring occasionally.

NOTE *Leftover potatoes can also be sautéd if you have some from another meal.*

If you prefer fried fish, try to serve it with boiled, baked or mashed potato; and space out fried fish by having it once every two or three weeks.

FRIDAY

Grapes with cream

bunch of black or green grapes or both
single cream (left over from another recipe)

1. Cut grapes in half lengthways and remove seeds.
2. Put into bowls and pour cream over the top.

NOTE *Keep 2 grapes for garnishing the evening salad.*

Tomato salad with stuffed eggs

2 eggs
1 teaspoon salad cream or mayonnaise (low calorie)
1 teaspoon natural yogurt (if available)
pinch curry powder
salt and black pepper
2 tablespoons oil
2 tablespoons wine or cider vinegar
finely chopped chives (optional)
1 tablespoon cream (if available)
2 grapes (if available)
1 large or 2 medium sized tomatoes
1 inch cucumber (optional)

1. Hard boil the eggs. To save on fuel, turn off the heat 2 minutes earlier than usual and leave in the hot water for about 5 minutes.
2. Plunge into cold water; peel the eggs and cut in half.
3. Remove the yolk and place in a cup or small bowl. Mix with the salad cream or mayonnaise and yogurt. Add curry powder and season to taste with salt.
4. Replace the yolk mixture in the egg.
   If possible, pipe in the mixture with a wide nozzle, and put the eggs aside while preparing the salad and dressing.

FRIDAY

5 For the dressing, mix together oil, vinegar and cream (if available) with seasoning and chopped chives.

6 Finely slice tomatoes and cucumber (optional) and arrange in a small bowl with a layer of cucumber between 2 layers of tomatoes. Garnish with the eggs and with 4 halves of deseeded grapes from lunch. Spoon over up to half the dressing.

7 Serve salad and eggs with brown or — for a change — a pitta bread warmed in the toaster.

NOTE *For Monday's salad, keep the remaining half of the salad dressing in the fridge.*

SATURDAY

Neck of lamb with lentils, peas and potato layer

1lb neck of lamb
1½ pints water or vegetable stock
stick of celery
1 leek
2oz/55g dried split peas
2oz/55g lentils
2 potatoes
seasoning

1. Wash, roughly chop and rewash the leek and celery.
2. Wash and drain the peas and lentils, removing black ones and odd bits.
3. Cover the lamb with cold water in a large pan and boil on the stove for 2-3 minutes, to remove impurities.
4. Remove lamb, wash under the cold tap.
5. Put lamb into clean ovenproof pan (with lid).
6. Add prepared celery, leek, peas and lentils with the stock or water and seasoning.
7. Bring to the boil; then place in the oven at about 350°F/180°C Gas 4 with a tight fitting lid.
8. Cook for at least 1 hour.
9. Wash or peel potatoes and finely slice. Place on top of lamb casserole after checking it's not getting too dry. Add more water or stock if necessary. Replace lid and cook for 20 minutes.
10. Remove lid and cook until potatoes are browned, meat is tender and peas and lentils are soft – about 15-20 minutes.
11. When serving, remove fat from lamb.

NOTE *This is an ideal dish to cook when entertaining, as it doesn't spoil easily.*

If cooking the apple tart at the same time, turn the oven up to 400°F/200°C/Gas 6 when the lid is removed from the casserole.

SATURDAY

Baked apple tart

For filling:
2 Bramleys or other cooking apples
½ oz margarine
½ oz caster or brown sugar
slice of lemon
juice of ⅛ lemon

For pastry:
4oz flour (half-white/half-brown)
2oz margarine (polyunsaturated)
2oz caster sugar
1 egg yolk
1 tablespoon milk

Filling

1. Wash, peel (if desired), core and slice the apples.
2. Put apples into water with a slice of lemon to prevent browning.
3. Preheat small pan and then add the margarine, lemon juice, drained apples and sugar.
4. Cover with a tight fitting lid and cook quickly to a pulp for about 5 minutes. Stir occasionally. Cool the apple.

Pastry

1. Sieve the flour. With the finger tips blend in the soft margarine. Add the caster sugar.
2. Make a well in the centre, add half the egg yolk and milk. Combine to make a paste, with as little handling as possible.
3. Select a small ovenproof plate or dish.
4. Split the pastry roughly in half. Roll out the smallest half on a floured work surface, to the size of the plate.
5. Place rolled pastry on the plate and then add apple pulp in the centre.
6. Brush edges of pastry with milk.
7. Roll out remaining pastry slightly larger than the size of plate and cover the apple.
8. Press edges of pastry together with a fork or knife handle.

SATURDAY

9. Make a slit in the centre of the pastry to allow steam to escape. Brush over with remaining half egg yolk.
10. Place on a baking tray and bake at 400°F/200°C/Gas 6 for about 25 minutes until the pastry is lightly browned and crisp.

NOTE *For variation, add 2 tablespoons raisins or a pinch of mixed spice or cinnamon.*
Keep egg white for Sunday's Cheese soufflé rarebit.

Baked sweetcorn with cheese sauce

2 cobs of sweetcorn with leaves
2oz cheese (see note)
1-2 tablespoons oil
1 tablespoon wine or cider vinegar
seasoning
1 dessertspoon chopped parsley or other fresh herbs (tarragon, chives)

1. Tie the leaves around the cobs to protect the flesh. Put cobs on a baking tray.
2. Bake for 20 minutes in the oven with the neck of lamb and the tart (or any other dish you are baking).
3. If you wish, remove flesh from the cobs after roasting.
4. Combine grated cheese, oil, vinegar, pepper, parsley and herbs.
5. Pour sauce over the cobs which can be eaten hot or cold. Serve with wholemeal bread or toast.

NOTE *Blue cheese (eg Stilton or Danish blue) makes this dish particularly tasty and colourful.*

SUNDAY

Roast chicken with braised celery, parsnips and gravy

3lb chicken
¾ pint chicken stock
1 garlic clove
seasoning
vegetable trimmings
3 sticks celery
½lb parsnips
1 teaspoon flour

1. Remove wings and legs (thigh and drumsticks) from the chicken and the bag of giblets, if present.
2. To make stock: simmer giblets in 1 pint water to make ¾ pint stock; simmer for ½ hour in pan with a lid. Alternatively use ¾ pint boiling water with stock cube.
3. Place vegetable trimmings in the bottom of a small roasting dish, and put the chicken on top, lightly seasoned and with the optional garlic clove in the cavity.
4. Roast at 400°F/200°C/Gas 6 for about 1 hour until cooked.
5. Meanwhile clean celery and remove stringy bits with a potato peeler (so it cooks quicker). Cut into slices a good ½ inch long.
6. Put celery in a small casserole dish with lid (tin foil will do for a lid). Add ¼ pint of the chicken stock and braise for 20 minutes in the oven along with the roasting chicken.
7. Also wash or peel the parsnips. Cut into even-sized wedges and braise in stock for 20 minutes or until cooked, as for the celery.
8. When the chicken is cooked, place on a carving dish.
9. Add remaining ¼ pint of chicken stock to the vegetable trimmings and a teaspoon of flour, mixed with a little cold water or stock.

SUNDAY

10 Stir over the stove until bubbling and slightly thickened, to make the gravy.
11 Retain one chicken breast for Tuesday's salad and carve the remaining meat to serve with vegetables and gravy.

NOTE *Celery and parsnips can be braised in vegetable stock saved from boiling vegetables.*

Use uncooked chicken wings as a basis for Monday evening's soup and the uncooked legs for stuffing and roasting for mid-day on Monday.

Leftover cooked breast is used for the salad on Tuesday evening.

The cooked carcass is also used for Monday's soup.

Baked rice pudding with jam

1oz/30g pudding rice
⅔ pint milk
drop vanilla essence
pinch of cinnamon
1 dessertspoon caster or brown sugar
2 teaspoons raspberry or other favourite jam

1 Bring rice, essence, milk and sugar to the boil on the stove.
2 Pour into a baking dish, sprinkle with cinnamon. Bake for ½ hour until rice is soft
(in the oven with the chicken).
3 Serve with a teaspoon of jam.

SUNDAY

Cheese soufflé rarebit

8 tablespoons milk
1 heaped teaspoon cornflour
½ teaspoon dry mustard
1 tablespoon cider or milk
1½ oz grated/crumbled Cheddar cheese
1 teaspoon dried herbs
2 eggs separated
1 egg white (see note)
salt and pepper
4 slices wholemeal toast

1. Heat oven to 400° F/200° C/Gas 6.
2. Bring milk to the boil in a small pan on the stove, while blending cornflour and mustard with the cider or remaining tablespoon of milk.
3. Pour blended flour mixture into boiling milk and stir thoroughly. Simmer for 2 minutes until thickened, stirring occasionally.
4. Turn off the heat and add Cheddar, herbs and 1 egg yolk, stirring well. Leave to stand while whisking 3 egg whites in a small basin until stiff.
5. Fold egg whites into the sauce and season to taste.
6. Pile mixture onto 4 slices of toast and brown in the oven on a baking tray for about 10 minutes.

NOTE *Keep 1 egg yolk for Monday's Stuffed chicken legs. The cooked rarebit can be kept in the fridge for the next day with half the egg whites – but not whisked. When required, the rarebit can be warmed on the stove, and the egg whites whisked as before.*

MONDAY

Chicken legs stuffed with herbs and sausagemeat
Baked potatoes and green salad

2 chicken legs raw from Sunday's joint
3oz sausagemeat
1 egg yolk
pinch of tarragon, chervil and parsley
seasoning
oil
2 baking potatoes

1 Mix sausagemeat, egg yolk and herbs together to make a stuffing.
2 Separate the chicken leg on the joint between the thigh and drumstick.
3 Take the drumstick and using flat edge of knife rub against the bone pushing the flesh downwards. When the flesh has been pushed

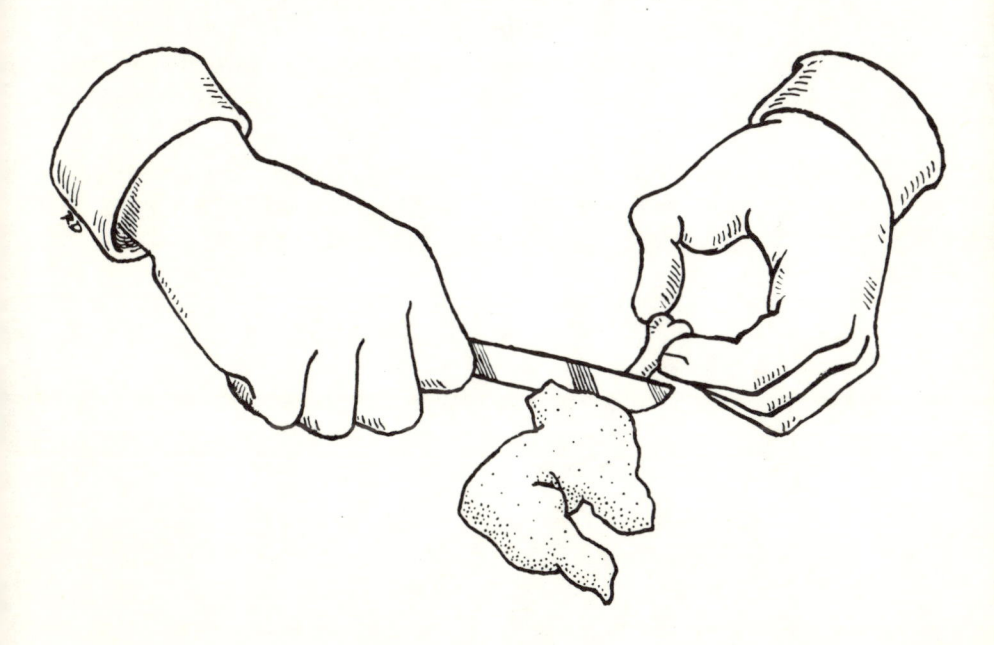

MONDAY

away, hit the end of the drumstick with the flat edge of a larger knife to break it away from the joint. This enables you to remove the drumstick without piercing the skin of the leg.

4 When the bone is loose, slip it out and stuff the cavity with the sausagemeat filling.

5 Lightly season both the drumsticks and thighs with black pepper and a little salt. Brush them lightly with oil and place on a baking tray.

6 Roast in the oven at 400°F/200°C/Gas 6 for about 40 minutes until crispy and cooked.

7 At the same time, skewer potatoes lengthwise and cook with chicken legs for at least 40 minutes, until soft.

8 Serve with green salad made from leftover salad ingredients and the dressing made for Friday's salad.

NOTE *When traditional salad vegetables become expensive, experiment with finely chopped raw sprouts and cabbage. Chinese Leaf lasts well and is economical. Steamed leeks and marrow also make a nice salad with oil and vinegar dressing.*

For colourful salads, grated carrot, swede and turnip are useful, or finely chopped red cabbage. The cabbage can be lightly cooked if chewing is a problem. Also try tinned sweetcorn.

MONDAY

Fruit en papillote

1 banana, 1 satsuma or fruit in season
dash of brandy (if available)
2 tablespoons natural yogurt
2 flat tablespoons demerara or brown sugar

1. Oil 2 square pieces of greaseproof paper.
2. Peel and slice the banana in half.
3. Peel the satsuma and separate segments.
4. Arrange half the fruit on each piece of paper, sprinkled with sugar and brandy.
5. Fold the papers round the fruit in the shape of a Cornish pasty.

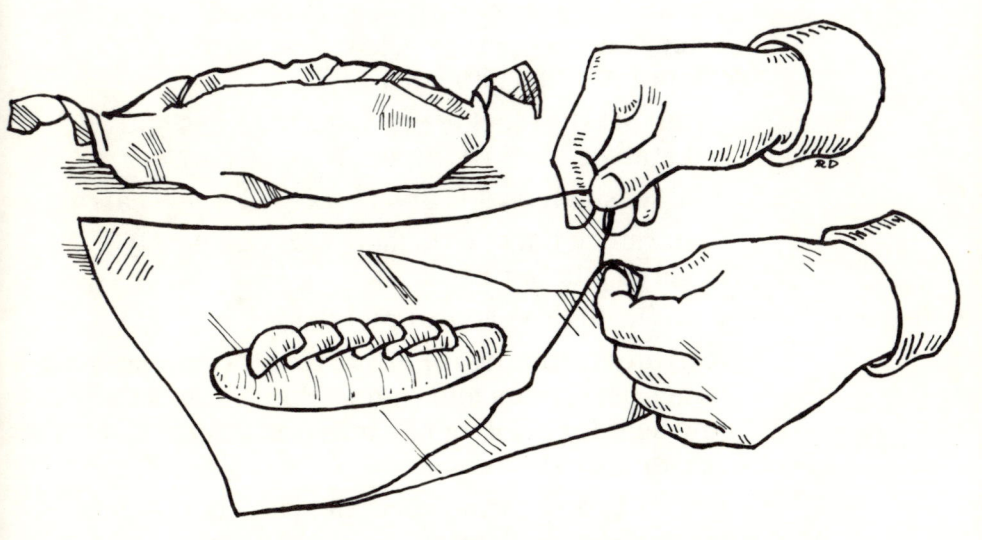

6. Bake in the oven with the roasting stuffed chicken legs for 10 minutes until the paper has puffed up and the fruit is soft.
7. Pour off the juice. Mix with the yogurt and spoon over the fruit in 2 dessert bowls.

NOTE *A dash of any spirit or liquor, sherry or cider that's stored away can be used to liven up this dish.*

MONDAY

Creamed carrot soup with grated Cheddar cheese

raw chicken wings from Sunday joint
chicken carcass from Sunday
1 onion peeled and chopped
1 stick celery washed and sliced
1½ pint water
6 peppercorns or black pepper
½ lb carrots
pinch of thyme
small carton double cream (see note)
2oz Cheddar cheese grated

1. Boil chicken carcass, wings, chopped onion, celery and peppercorns in the water for 25 minutes in a pan with a lid.
2. Drain off the stock, remove the carcass and vegetables. Return the stock to the pan.
3. Add washed, peeled and rewashed sliced carrots.
4. Bring stock back to the boil and cook gently in a covered pan for 20 minutes.
5. Pass through a sieve or blender.
6. Add any trimmings of meat from the carcass and wings, the cream and thyme. Simmer on a very low heat for a further 10 minutes. Adjust seasoning to taste.
7. Pour into dishes and sprinkle with cheese, serve with wholemeal bread.

NOTE *Long-life cream may be cheaper, or look for one reduced for a quick sale.*

TUESDAY

Macaroni cheese with peppers and bacon
Peas and cabbage

2-3oz red and green pepper (see note)
3oz Cheddar cheese (reduced fat)
2 rashers smoked back bacon
3oz/85g wholewheat macaroni
1oz margarine (polyunsaturated)
1oz flour
½ pint milk (semi-skimmed)
½ teaspoon prepared mustard
pinch paprika
peas, cabbage (4-6 oz of each)

1. Slice the tops off a red and a green pepper and dice the tops.
2. Grate the cheese and chop the bacon into slithers.
3. Cook the macaroni in boiling water until swollen and soft.
4. Melt the margarine in a pan, add the diced pepper to soften for 2-3 minutes.
5. Stir in the flour and cook for a further minute.
6. Remove the pan from the heat and stir in the milk gradually. Return to the heat and bring to the boil, stirring continuously.
7. Cook for a minute, adding the mustard and paprika. Remove from heat and add half grated cheese, stirring until cheese has melted.
8. Add cooked macaroni to sauce. Pour into a casserole dish or 2 individual ones.
9. Top with remaining grated cheese and bacon slithers. Brown under grill, and check that bacon is cooked.
10. Cook the vegetables in the minimum amount of water so they are slightly crisp.

TUESDAY

NOTE *Peppers can be used during the next few days for stuffing. To prepare stuffing, buy offcuts of cold meat or bacon and combine with rice and herbs.*

Grilled grapefruit

1 pink grapefruit
1 tablespoon demerara or brown sugar
2 dessertspoons sherry (if available)

1. Cut washed grapefruit in half across the segments and loosen each segment away from the pith. Cut around the core in the centre and remove.
2. Sprinkle grapefruit halves with sugar and sherry, if used.
3. Grill under hot grill until lightly browned.

Cold chicken with cucumber yogurt salad

chicken breast from Sunday joint
½ clove garlic (optional)
¼ cucumber
2-3 teaspoons lemon juice
3 tablespoons natural yogurt
black pepper
1 dessertspoon chopped fresh mint or dill (optional)
tomato for decoration

1. Chop garlic very small.
2. Finely slice washed cucumber.
3. Mix cucumber, garlic, yogurt, black pepper, lemon juice and herbs together. Cool in fridge for an hour.
4. Place salad on a plate and top with chicken and decorate with a slice of tomato.
Serve with brown bread.